YOUTH BIBLE STUDY GUIDE
Money and Giving

Youth Bible Study Guides

YOUTH BIBLE STUDY GUIDE
Money and Giving

COMPILED AND WRITTEN BY
CHIP AND HELEN KENDALL

Authentic

First published 2014 by Authentic Media Ltd
Presley Way, Crownhill, Milton Keynes, MK8 0ES.
www.authenticmedia.co.uk

British Library Cataloguing in Publication Data
A catalogue record for this book is available from the British Library

ISBN-13: 978-1-86024-638-8

Extracts taken from:
Keith Tondeur, *Street Parables*, Authentic, 2004
Andy Flannagan, *God 360°*, Spring Harvest and Authentic, 2006
Chip Kendall, *The Mind of chipK: Enter at Your Own Risk*, Authentic, 2005
Jenny Baker, *Vibrant Spirituality*, Spring Harvest and Authentic, 2004
Sharon Witt, *Teen Talk*, Authentic, 2011
Krish Kandiah, *Twenty-Four: Integrating Faith and Real Life*, Authentic, 2008
Peter Meadows and Joseph Steinberg, *The Book of Y*, Authentic, 2007

Cover and page design by Temple Design
Cover based on a design by Beth Ellis
Printed in Great Britain by Bell and Bain, Glasgow

'Give to others, and you will receive. You will be given much. It will be poured into your hands – more than you can hold. You will be given so much that it will spill into your lap. The way you give to others is the way God will give to you.'

(Luke 6:38)

Chip and Helen Kendall are Creative Arts Pastors at Audacious Church, Manchester, and also love spending as much time as possible with their kids, Cole, Eden and Elliot. They currently reside in Stockport, England and they still have trouble understanding each other's accents.

Chip tours the world, fronting the Chip Kendall Band. His album *Holy Freaks* and first book *The Mind of chipK: Enter at Your Own Risk* have helped loads of young people grow in their faith. He's also the driving force behind a new youth media movement called MYvoice with Cross Rhythms, as well as being a regular presenter on GodTV. All of these jobs continue to pave the way for him to speak at events everywhere. www.chipkendall.com

After working for ten years as a dancer and tour/bookings manager, Helen now juggles looking after the kids with her work at Audacious Church helping to develop dance and all things creative. She also enjoys doing some writing and project management. Helen loves the variety in her life, and no two days are ever the same.

Thank Yous

Massive thanks to Malcolm Down, Liz Williams and the rest of the gang at Authentic Media for giving us the opportunity to work on these study guides . . . it's been a blast. Thanks to everyone at Audacious Church for being an amazing church family. Thanks to lovely Lucy West for the fantastic photos. To everyone who talked to Chip for the 'people clips', thanks for your honesty and willingness to put up with the quirky questions. A really huge thank you to Brian and Norma Wilson for their 'hidden pearls' of wisdom. We loved your perspective on things. Finally, big thanks to all the authors whose work we have used in this book. You are an inspiration.

CONTENTS

INSTRUCTIONS

The book you're holding in your hands is a study guide. It's a compilation of extracts from lots of other books written about this subject. It might not make you the world's expert on the subject, but it should give you lots of useful information and, even better, it should give you some idea of what the Bible has to say about . . . MONEY AND GIVING.

What is a 'reaction box'?

Throughout the book, you'll find these helpful little reaction boxes. We've added them so that you can decide for yourself what you think about what you've just read. Here's what one should look like once you've filled it in:

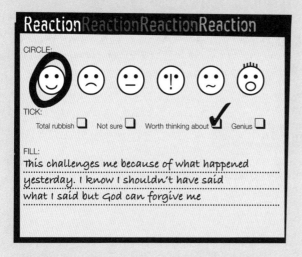

Pretty simple really . . .

Circle the face that reflects how you feel about it.

Tick the box that shows what you think about it.

Fill in any thoughts you have about what you've learned on the lines provided.

What are 'people clips'?

Just so you don't get too bored, we've added a bunch of 'people clips' to each study guide. These are people just like you, who were happy for us to pick their brains about various related topics. Who knows? Maybe you'll find someone you recognize.

What are 'hidden pearls'?

Everyone needs some good old-fashioned 'grandparently' advice, so we collected some pearls of wisdom from our friends Brian and Norma Wilson, which you can find scattered throughout the book.

What is a 'reality check'?

Finally, throughout the book you will come across sections called 'reality check'. These should provide a chance for you to apply what you've been learning to your own life experiences.

Other than that, the only rule that applies when reading this book is that you HAVE FUN! So start reading.

Chip & Helen

Introduction

> So be sure to give to the poor. Don't hesitate to give to them, because the LORD your God will bless you for doing this good thing. He will bless you in all your work and in everything you do.

(Deuteronomy 15:10)

Think the hottest topics in the Bible are things like healing and prayer? You might be surprised to hear that there are more references to money than to either of these activities throughout the Scriptures. Topics relating to money, gold, wealth and finance are mentioned hundreds and hundreds of times throughout the Bible. That's because God knows how important they are to us! You might have lots of money or you might be super-skint. Either way, it's clear God definitely doesn't want you avoiding the subject!

This book focuses particularly on one aspect of our finances – *giving*. It's literally where the rubber meets the road in your faith walk in terms of 'putting your money where your mouth is'. If you say you are a Christian and you've given God your life, surely this has to have an impact on how you use your money and how you give. Does God have access to your bank account or are you happy to give him your time, passion and energy but want to keep your hard-earned pennies for yourself?

Giving is a journey: it is both a lifelong decision and a day by day challenge. We hope all the extracts you read in this book will help you to make up your mind about what God is saying to you about giving, ownership and finance. Remember, you can't buy salvation, or forgiveness, or get yourself into God's 'good books' by giving – that's not what it's about. If you've become a Christian then all that is sorted. Giving is about living life to the full, learning to trust God in practical ways and obey him even when it doesn't always make logical sense. Giving can reward you with some amazing experiences of God's faithfulness, both to you and to others, and you will find yourself impacted by giving just as much as receiving. So let's see what the Bible has to say about . . . MONEY AND GIVING.

Money, Money, Money

Each one of you should give what you have decided in your heart to give. You should not give if it makes you unhappy or if you feel forced to give. God loves those who are happy to give.

(2 Corinthians 9:7)

1

First up

We thought that at the start of a book on giving it might be best to get right down to the reasons we usually don't want to give. If we can all get over those hurdles then the rest of the book will make more sense. So before we go on to talk about tithes, offerings, giving to the poor and all that, let's take a look at 'ownership'.

We live in a society where we have a lot of rights. We have our human rights, our family rights, our rights as citizens and our consumer rights. We feel like we deserve quite a lot out of life and, if we're not careful, this can affect the way we see *our* stuff and *our* money. We feel like we *own* our money and our things.

We earned it. We bought it. It's ours. Our *right*. And that is totally true from one perspective . . .

But if you look at it another way, we wouldn't have anything if it wasn't for the opportunities we've been given. We live in a country where we get a free education and free healthcare, but what if those opportunities were taken away? What if we had been born into a poor family in India, where we had to go out to work from the age of 6 and never got the chance to go to school?

When we take a step back out of our culture, our life, what we expect, we can start to see that God has given us the opportunities we have. He gives us talents. He opens doors for jobs and pocket money, etc. If we can get out of the mentality of 'everything is mine' and change it to 'everything is God's' then we will actually be happier, more free and more able to enjoy what we have – and to give what we have.

This first Life Lesson is full of extracts about people who clung on to their money and hoarded it up in the mistaken hope that it would make them happy. As you read, think about what your attitude is towards your money and your stuff. Think about how much you take for granted or assume you have a right to. Then thank God for the things he has put in your hands and ask him what he wants you to do with them.

Banking
on Wealth

Read Luke 18:18–30

A banker was praying. He had been a Christian for as long as he could remember and always attended church on Sundays. He had a quiet time every day, he tithed, and on special occasions he even fasted. But he had been troubled for some time, so he plucked up courage and asked Jesus, 'What must I do to fully receive eternal life?'

As he listened in silence he heard a still, small voice: 'You know my commandments – do not kill, commit adultery, steal or lie. Have you obeyed them?'

'I have kept all these commandments since I was a child,' the banker replied.

'There is one thing I need to ask you to do, though,' said Jesus. 'Where do you place your security? In worldly terms you are so rich. **WHY NOT SHOW THAT YOU TRUST ME BY SELLING EVERYTHING YOU HAVE AND GIVING THE PROCEEDS TO THE POOR?** Then you will be storing up treasures you can never lose – treasures in heaven.'

The banker felt as though he'd been shot. Surely he wasn't meant to do this? Surrender all the money he'd worked hard to acquire? Ask his family to adjust to a simpler lifestyle, a smaller house and an older car? For the sake of the poor? He wasn't sure whether he wanted to pay the cost of following Jesus that closely.

As God watches us wrestling with these issues, he must reflect on how hard it is for wealthy people to really surrender everything to him. He must be sad as he thinks of how many people in the affluent countries aren't truly worshipping him because they are too committed to possessions. He sympathizes with them but wishes they could understand that those who take that difficult step will never regret it. After all, they would get not only thanks on earth, but eternal treasure.

Keith Tondeur, *Street Parables*, Authentic Media, 2004

Reaction Reaction Reaction Reaction

CIRCLE:

TICK:
Total rubbish ☐ Not sure ☐ Worth thinking about ☐ Genius ☐

FILL:

....

....

....

....

How Much
Do You Trust Him?

Helen talks

I know I'm not alone in always finding the Bible story in the last extract a bit of a scary one. It's one of those that you slightly want to skip over and pretend you didn't notice! In the previous extract God told a banker to give all his money to the poor. In the Bible he's talking to a rich young ruler, someone probably equivalent to a footballer or actor today. Imagine if Simon Cowell or David Beckham suddenly sold all their houses and cars and everything they owned and gave all the money away . . . They could probably feed some African countries all by themselves!

Maybe you aren't quite as rich as Simon Cowell or David Beckham but, still, the thought of giving away everything you own sends a bit of a shiver down your spine. Why do you think that is? I am talking to myself here, too, because I haven't got this sorted out, but I think it all boils down to one thing: we don't trust God enough.

What does money give us? It gives us security. If we have money we will be able to pay for a house to live in, a university course, a car to drive. It gives us the ability to do things such as pay for flights, take a year out travelling, go on trips, buy cinema tickets and go to watch our favourite football team. With money, we have the ability to purchase clothes, computer games, phones, iPads . . . and the list goes on. And all those things are good – don't get me wrong. It's important to have somewhere warm and dry to live. It's fantastic to be able to do stuff, learn stuff and experience new things. And owning things isn't necessarily bad either. **WHAT IS BAD IS THAT WE DON'T *TRUST* GOD WITH ALL THAT**.

If God is supposed to be our loving Father and we've given him everything, why is it that we still think we would end up living on the streets, never be able to do anything fun, and have nothing?

Imagine this:

What if your mum or dad was having trouble paying the mortgage and they were about to lose the house. If you sold everything you had and gave them the money, would they just pocket it and then chuckle to themselves as they jetted off on a nice holiday leaving you homeless? No, they would pay the mortgage debt and then lavish gratitude on you, and they would want to bless you back. They would look after you and make sure you had everything you needed, to the best of their ability.

Now I'm not suggesting that God is really skint and can't afford to look after all the poor people in the world – but you get the picture. **GOD OFTEN WANTS US TO BE THE SOLUTION TO THE WORLD'S PROBLEMS**, and when we are obedient to him, he will look after us.

Scary stuff! I've never given away everything I own, but I've heard stories of people who have. And you know what? God has always given back to them and blessed them more than they could imagine.

ReactionReactionReactionReaction

CIRCLE:

☺ ☹ 😐 😦 🙂 😲

TICK:

Total rubbish ☐   Not sure ☐   Worth thinking about ☐   Genius ☐

FILL:

....
....
....
....

Me, Me, Me

Read Luke 12:16–21.

A rich industrialist had had an excellent year and got an enormous bonus. He thought to himself, 'How am I going to spend this? I work so hard that I am perfectly justified in spending this on myself.'

Then he thought, 'I know what I will do. I will buy another large house in the country, just in case I ever get a day off. I will furnish it with expensive ornaments and the most extravagant furnishings I can buy. I will purchase a new top-of-the-range convertible with my own personalized number plate. I could even afford a private jet. This would be very useful because I am such an important person and it would help me to get around all my businesses quicker. Then I will be able to look around and say to myself, "Look at what I have achieved." I have got so much here, I really will be able to enjoy myself in the years ahead. One day, I keep promising myself, I will take life easy. I will drink, eat and be merry.'

But the man lived like a fool. He lived just for himself. He lived as if his life would go on forever. But that night he died.

So what would now happen to all the things he had so selfishly stored up for his future use?

The message of this story is clear. This is how it is going to be for everyone who hoards things for themselves and ignores God's teaching and the desperate needs of others.

Jesus strongly disapproves of all actions that have underlying selfish motives. He also teaches that just having more will never in itself truly satisfy. Just because we have more money it does not mean that our lives will be any better. In fact there is ample evidence to suggest that really rich people live increasingly isolated and unfulfilled lives. The more possessions we have, the more time, money and effort it takes to maintain them. So both God and others get squeezed out. After all, if we started really applying God's teaching or caring about the poor, we might have to get rid of the very things we covet so much. So we keep on accumulating until one day, while we are still blissfully unaware, our possessions start possessing us! In this particular parable the rich man can only talk to himself about what he feels he has achieved. Nobody else is pleased or interested. In fact he is likely to have many enemies, as he seems not to have shared his good fortune with anyone else.

In today's society this would be seen as a 'success story'. This man would be regarded as a key player; he would appear regularly in the media and at conferences; he would be a well-known name. **JESUS CALLED HIM A FOOL, NOT BECAUSE OF HIS SUCCESS BUT BECAUSE OF HIS WRONG PRIORITIES.** As Christians we are called to be in the world but not of it, not to be so absorbed by our possessions that they and we become one and the same. So this story is a clear warning to us. Jesus is telling us to stop concentrating on things on earth because they are trivial. He pleads with us not to be so focused on ourselves.

Look again at the parable. It's all 'I', 'myself' and 'my'. Surely this man has not achieved all this by himself. Where is the mention of his workers, his suppliers or his customers? How about others who have been involved in his life – his parents, teachers, trainers? Where is God in his thinking? The answer, sadly, is that the rich fool brings no one else in to the equation. He believes it is his talent alone that has enabled him to be so successful and so he concentrates purely on 'self' – the rudest four-letter word in the English language.

Keith Tondeur, *Street Parables*, Authentic Media, 2004

Reaction ReactionReactionReaction

CIRCLE:

TICK:

Total rubbish ☐   Not sure ☐   Worth thinking about ☐   Genius ☐

FILL:

....
....
....
....

The Greater Blessing

Chip talks

When's the last time you gave something away?

I don't mean something little. I don't even necessarily just mean money. I mean, when's the last time you actually gave something away – something you genuinely treasured – and had no expectation of receiving anything back in return?

How did it make you feel?

In Acts 20:35 we read the words of the apostle Paul:

> I always showed you that you should work just as I did and help people who are weak. I taught you to remember the words of the Lord Jesus: 'It is a greater blessing to give than to receive.'

I know without a doubt that the times I've truly sacrificed my own ambitions, dug deep, and given something away, this verse has proved to be true for me over and over again. I've come away from the experience surprised by how great it felt to give, and I've been more blessed in the giving than in the getting.

Once, I sensed the Lord telling me to give away my prized hoodie. I literally cried my eyes out afterwards as I thought, 'What have I just done?!' But the results of that simple act of obedience have been absolutely overwhelming. There isn't enough space here to tell the whole story, but needless to say I've been extremely blessed as a result of that one simple act of generosity. It was like a seed sown in faith, and the harvest is still coming in!

If you stop to think about it, **EVERYTHING WE HAVE BELONGS TO GOD ANYWAY**. He blesses us with time, money and possessions in order to see what kind of stewards we will be. There's a difference between owning something and allowing that thing to 'own' you. To give it away is the ultimate indication that it doesn't own you. That's part of the reason we are more blessed in the giving than in the getting. We become a channel through which God can bless others, and we get to enjoy taking part as well. It's a win, win, win situation all round!

Go for the greater blessing. Give generously and watch what God does.

Questions to consider:

• *What has God blessed me with?*

• *How could I be a blessing to others in giving this away?*

• *How is my generous giving like making an investment?*

• *What are some of the results I can expect if I give with a good heart? (HINT: Check out Luke 6:38)*

ReactionReactionReactionReaction

CIRCLE:

TICK:

Total rubbish ☐   Not sure ☐   Worth thinking about ☐   Genius ☐

FILL:

....

....

....

....

Name: **Georgia Pennells**

Age: **17**

Town: **Manchester**

What do you want to do when you grow up?

Dancing! And youth work.

How many bubbles are there in a glass of Coke?

92

That's not many. Is it a small glass?

Yeah, definitely! I can't drink too much because I can't burp.

How many animals did Moses take on the ark?

Moses didn't take any on the ark! He wasn't even born then.

(Correct! You pass ☺)

When is the last time you saw a bee?

um, I don't know what to say . . .

That's okay! Now a more serious question . . . If you could be more generous than anyone in the world, who would you like to out-give?

The most generous person in the world.

Have you ever been forced to give away something you didn't want to give away?

Yes. Since I wasn't spending enough time practising playing my piano, my parents basically 'suggested' I give it away!

Earth is Just Our Temporary Resting Place

Then Jesus used this story: 'There was a rich man who had some land. His land grew a very good crop of food. He thought to himself, "What will I do? I have no place to keep all my crops." Then he said, "I know what I will do. I will tear down my barns and build bigger barns! I will put all my wheat and good things together in my new barns. Then I can say to myself, I have many good things stored. I have saved enough for many years. Rest, eat, drink and enjoy life!" But God said to that man, "Foolish man! Tonight you will die. So what about the things you prepared for yourself? Who will get those things now?" This is how it will be for anyone who saves things only for himself. To God that person is not rich.'

(Luke 12:16–21)

The world is a bridge. The wise man will pass over it but will not build his house upon it. We all need to remind ourselves constantly that our time on earth is but a stepping-stone to the next world that awaits us. This is the reason why we are here in the first place. But we all continue disastrously to suffer stress, debt and breakdowns in the idle pursuit of temporary pleasures. The tragedy of this story in Luke is that the impending death of the rich man is only reminding us of something that we already know:

his soul is already dead. By concentrating on money and things rather than God and people we are dying as we live. Knowing God and loving and being loved by others is real treasure. We need to remember that the instant that death occurs, the narrow gap between us and our possessions becomes an unbridgeable chasm.

Even as Christians we can measure success by title, wealth or house. People even seek to express their own importance and immortality by having a personalized number plate on their car! Yet the more we have, the more anxious and dissatisfied we become. Everything needs to be bigger, newer and certainly better than our neighbours. It is so easy to blame our materialistic culture, but if we behave selfishly it is our own responsibility.

Keith Tondeur, *Street Parables*, Authentic Media, 2004

ReactionReactionReactionReaction

CIRCLE:

TICK:
Total rubbish ☐   Not sure ☐   Worth thinking about ☐   Genius ☐

FILL:

....
....
....
....

Attitude of
Gratitude

Helen talks

Do you ever feel like you are just a bit short on cash? Not got quite the most up-to-date phone? Driving an old banger instead of the sweet ride your mate was given for their 18th birthday? It's easy to feel like we don't really have enough to be thankful for and that if we had just a little bit more, we would be really happy.

In fact, if we wait for the right stuff to arrive in our lives before we are happy, we will never get there. There will always be a more up-to-date whatever it is, and someone else will always have something better than us. There have been loads of studies done on what amount of money makes people feel happy and feel as though they have enough. But no matter what they earn, most people think they would be happy if they earned just a bit more.

THE BEST WAY TO FEEL RICH, SATISFIED AND CONTENT IS TO BE THANKFUL! In reality, most of us have an awful lot to be thankful for and gratitude is an attitude and state of mind that we can decide to take into every situation. It's our choice.

Jewish people have prayers of thanksgiving and blessing written into their daily lives. They discipline themselves to recite them as a regular habit. There are prayers to pray as they wash their hands, blessings over bread, blessings and thanks over their meals, and thanksgiving blessings over the different parts of their prayer garments. There is even a prayer of blessing and thanks to God for their bodily functions that they pray while they're on the toilet!

We live in a society where the marketers and retailers will always have us believing that we need more 'stuff' in order to be happy. Don't buy into it. They only want your money! Making a decision to thank God for every small thing you have, regardless of whether you want a better one, will help you appreciate what you have. It will free you up to be generous and give stuff away, rather than grasping and holding on to everything you can get.

Psalm 116:7 says, 'My soul, relax! The LORD is caring for you.' God knows what we need and he will take care of us. Next time you start to feel that desperate urge for something new, take some time to thank God for what you have already. If you feel that nudge from the Holy Spirit to give something away that you think you can't do without, **REMEMBER GOD TAKES CARE OF YOU**. He sees it all. He knows what you want and what you need, and he is a generous and extravagant Father.

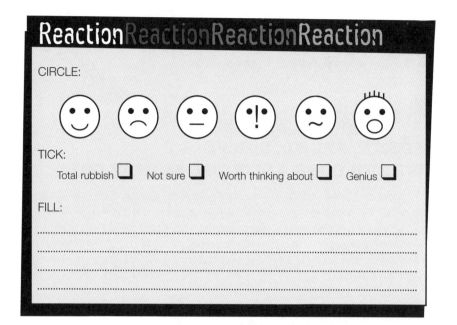

Reaction Reaction Reaction Reaction

CIRCLE:

TICK:

Total rubbish ☐   Not sure ☐   Worth thinking about ☐   Genius ☐

FILL:

....

....

....

....

Reality Check

SPEND, SPEND, SPEND . . . WHERE DOES ALL YOUR MONEY GO?

We know budgeting sounds like something your 80-year-old granny would go on about. But we want you to keep track of what you spend for two weeks, just so you can get an idea of how much money you get through and on what. We've designed this handy little table for you to fill in. You might want to keep a tally on a separate bit of paper and then fill in the total amount at the end of the week:

How do you spend your money?

Fill in the TOTAL amount you spent in a week on each of the following:	Week 1	Week 2
Essential food		
Bus fares		
Other essential items (i.e. you actually need them to live . . . not that you just really want them)		
Total spent on essentials		
Non-essential food (e.g. meals out with friends when you could have taken sandwiches, snacks such as chocolate and crisps)		
Drinks (e.g. coffees, fizzy drinks)		
Entertainment (tickets for stuff, entrance fees, bowling, football, etc.)		
Phone calls/texts		
Clothes		
Toys (any kind of entertainment, games, music, etc.)		
Anything else		
Total spent on non-essentials		

OK, so look at your total expenditure on essential and non-essential purchases. Are you surprised at how much money you get through?

Now fill in the mini-table below for the same two weeks:

	Week 1	Week 2
Non-essential spending		
Saving		
Giving		

Just take some time to look at those numbers and think about these facts:*

- 80% of humanity lives on less than $10 per day (around £7)

- 20% of people in the world live on $1.25 per day (around 80p)

- In 1998 in the USA 8 billion dollars was spent on cosmetics; just 6 billion could have achieved basic education for all

- In 1998 11 billion dollars was spent on ice cream in Europe alone; 9 billion dollars could have achieved water and sanitation for everyone in the world

Do you think you are giving enough to help the needs of others?

Can you think of things you could cut back on to release some money to other people? The other reality checks in this book will give you some suggestions about how to do that.

All statistics from www.globalissues.org Poverty Facts and Stats

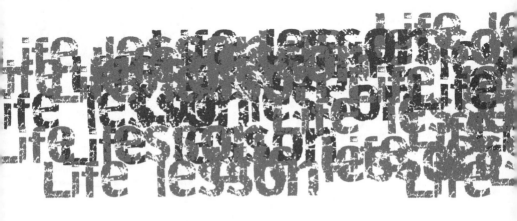

One For Me . . .
One For You . . .
One For Me . . .

The LORD All-Powerful says, 'Try this test. Bring one-tenth of your things to me. Put them in the treasury. Bring food to my house. Test me! If you do these things, I will surely bless you. Good things will come to you like rain falling from the sky. You will have more than enough of everything.'

(Malachi 3:10)

2

First up

While the advertisers try to tell you that more money and more stuff will make you happier, more successful and more secure, just a glance at the lives of the rich and famous often proves otherwise: drug use, depression, divorce and even suicide are all fairly common. What if the secret of a well-balanced life was actually to give away what you own? What if proving that you owned your possessions, rather than them owning you could actually lead to more peace of mind and security than a big bank balance?

Paul says in 2 Corinthians 9:7, 'Each one of you should give what you have decided in your heart to give. You should not give if it makes you unhappy or if you feel forced to give. God loves those who are happy to give.' The Bible talks a lot about tithes and offerings. A tithe is traditionally 10% of your income, and offerings are often seen as gifts that you give over and above the tithe. The main point to get your head around is that everything is God's – we are just the stewards of it. By giving, we are simply releasing back to God what is his, instead of clinging on to it for ourselves. If you had a tap in your house that was blocked and no water came out, then eventually you'd stop using that tap. So why should it be any different with giving? If the money God gives you always gets stuck with you and none of it finds its way out to other people, then you're severely limiting your usefulness to God in blessing others through you.

We think giving should be an exciting thing, a great part of the adventure of life with God. After all, you can't out-give God, it's impossible! Check out the verse in Malachi 3:10 again. In this Life Lesson we'll talk you through some of the nuts and bolts of giving and hopefully turn you into a regular and cheerful giver.

Tithes and Offerings

chipK's mind

All through the Bible, we find the people of God doing something slightly peculiar with their money. No matter how much or how little they earned, they would always give part of it back to God. The 'money' they gave him wasn't pounds and pence (duh) – it was usually a lamb or a goat or even a dove – but it still meant just as much to them back then as our currency means to us today. It was called their 'tithes and offerings', and this is still practised by Christians today.

All my life, I've given 10% of the money I've earned to my church as a tithe, and any money I've given on top of that was considered my 'offering'. Even when I was receiving just one dollar a week as my allowance, I would still faithfully give ten cents back to God, plus a small offering. It was a principle which my parents considered to be extremely important and it's stuck with me ever since.

Some people argue that it's not right to tithe. They say that God won't love you any less if you don't – and they're absolutely correct. If the only reason we're giving our tithes and offerings is because we feel obliged to, then God would rather that we didn't give at all. **HE WANTS US TO GIVE CHEERFULLY, KNOWING THAT HIS LOVE COMES FREE OF CHARGE.**

If it helps, think of it like this:

Tithing is giving back to God what's already his.

Offerings are gifts given in faith to the Giver of all we have. That's a lot of giving!

God's mind

Each one of you should give what you have decided in your heart to give. You should not give if it makes you unhappy or if you feel forced to give. God loves those who are happy to give.

(2 Corinthians 9:7)

'Give to others, and you will receive. You will be given much. It will be poured into your hands – more than you can hold. You will be given so much that it will spill into your lap. The way you give to others is the way God will give to you.'

(Luke 6:38)

People all around the country heard about this command. So the Israelites gave the first part of their harvest of grain, grapes, oil, honey and all the things they grew in their fields. They brought one-tenth of all these many things.

(2 Chronicles 31:5)

You made promises to God Most High, so give him what you promised.
Bring your sacrifices and thank offerings.

(Psalm 50:14)

I taught you to remember the words of the Lord Jesus:
'It is a greater blessing to give than to receive.'

(Acts 20:35b)

Your mind

Why is money so valuable to us?

....
....
....

Do tithes and offerings always have to be given in the form of money?

....
....
....

How faithfully do I tithe?

....
....
....

Why is it better to give than to get?

....
....
....

I will commit to giving God my tithes and offerings from the money I've earned by:

....
....
....

Chip Kendall, *The Mind of chipK: Enter at Your Own Risk*, Authentic Media, 2005

Reaction Reaction Reaction Reaction

CIRCLE:

TICK:

Total rubbish ☐   Not sure ☐   Worth thinking about ☐   Genius ☐

FILL:

....
....
....
....

More on Tithes

Helen talks

When Christians talk about a tithe, they usually mean giving 10% of their income. This was a commandment from God and is talked about a lot in the Old Testament, but the story of the first tithe is a bit of an obscure one, featuring a priest with a very funny name, 'Melchizedek'. In Genesis 14, Abram (soon to become Abraham) rescues his nephew Lot from capture and then is greeted by Melchizedek King of Salem, a priest of God Most High. This guy isn't mentioned before or after this story and many scholars believe he was actually a 'theophany' – an appearance of Jesus before his main time on earth. Anyway, Abram gives a tenth of everything he owns to Melchizedek in worship to God.

Some people believe that tithing is an Old Testament principle and that we don't have to do it now that Jesus has died for us and we are living under grace rather than under the law. It's true that we don't need to give in order to earn our way into heaven, but I think there are loads of reasons why giving regularly is really good for us:

- Giving *regularly* means you *regularly* have to trust God in a very tangible way.

- Tithing is totally countercultural. If you want a way to stand out as a Christian and show your friends that your life is different, then this is a good one.

- Giving regularly gets your focus off yourself and onto others, which is never a bad thing.

- Giving money helps other people.

- God says he will reward those who give – check out Luke 6:38: 'Give to others, and you will receive. You will be given much. It will be poured into your hands – more than you can hold. You will be given so much that it will spill into your lap. The way you give to others is the way God will give to you.'

Just one final thought to remember: you will seldom find that you're able to 'afford' to tithe! If you keep thinking to yourself, 'When I get a job I'll tithe,' or 'When my pocket money gets increased I'll tithe,' or 'When I get a pay rise I'll be able to afford it.' It will never happen! **YOU NEED TO MAKE A DECISION TO TRUST GOD AND HE WILL ALWAYS FILL IN THE GAPS.** The more you earn, the more things you will find to spend your money on. It's about making a decision to give back to God what is his, and trust him for the rest. It's a great adventure – I love it!

ReactionReactionReactionReaction

CIRCLE:

😊 😞 😐 😯 😌 😲

TICK:

Total rubbish ☐   Not sure ☐   Worth thinking about ☐   Genius ☐

FILL:

....

....

....

....

Hidden pearls

I think you've got to support your own church and then, after that, charities and societies that you believe in. We get a lot of requests for money from charities, and we support some that are Christian and some that are not.

Want to Be Rich?

Helen talks

Everybody wants to be rich, right? Maybe these verses hold the key to riches?!

God is the one who gives seed to those who plant, and he gives bread for food. And God will give you spiritual seed and make that seed grow. He will produce a great harvest from your goodness. God will make you rich in every way so that you can always give freely. And your giving through us will make people give thanks to God.

(2 Corinthians 9:10–11)

Y ou've got to admit, our society is very much 'me first'. We are focused on ourselves, meeting our own needs and getting as rich as we can. Of course we know we should throw the occasional bone someone else's way, but in general it's all about getting more to make ME happy. This verse points out that in God's kingdom, it's the other way round.

'God will make you rich in every way **SO THAT** you can always give freely' – not so that you can have the latest clothes or gadgets, or so that you can buy whatever you want or do whatever you want, but so that you can bless others. It's a whole shift in thinking, but **GOD WANTS US TO BE RICH SO THAT WE CAN BE GENEROUS**. That's not just rich in financial terms; it's spiritually rich, rich in relationships, rich in love, 'rich in every way'.

Why is generosity so important to God? The second part of the verse holds the key to this: 'And your giving through us will make people give thanks to God.' Our main purpose as Christians is to introduce other people to Jesus and to a lifestyle of giving thanks to God. Being generous is a great way to do this.

Some definitions of generosity are:

- *Giving without expecting anything in return*
- *Freedom from meanness or small-mindedness*
- *Readiness or bigheartedness in giving*

Generosity stands out against a 'me first' culture. It surprises people; it shows that you trust God rather than money; it demonstrates that your treasure is in heaven; it shows that God is in charge of your life rather than stuff or retailers. **GENEROSITY IS AMAZING AND GOD WILL BLESS GENEROSITY.**

Maybe you feel that you don't have enough to be generous, but why not plan your life and finances around enabling yourself to be generous? Instead of saving up money, or working for money to spend on yourself, save it up so that you will have the opportunity to be generous. Don't buy lunch once a week, buy it once a month and pay for a friend's lunch. Or miss out on a trip to the cinema and then pay for someone else's ticket. Or cut back on something for a few weeks because you know a missionary is coming to church, so you will be able to give something in the offering.

The exciting thing about generosity is that not only does it breed generosity from others, but God sees it. The verse that started us off says that 'God will give you spiritual seed and make that seed grow. He will produce a great harvest from your goodness.'

Read the whole of 2 Corinthians chapter 9 and write down some of the things that stand out to you about generosity and giving:

....

....

....

....

ReactionReactionReactionReaction

CIRCLE:

😊 😟 😐 😠 😕 😮

TICK:

Total rubbish ☐   Not sure ☐   Worth thinking about ☐   Genius ☐

FILL:

....

....

....

....

Name: Andy Terry

Age: 23

Town: Crewe

Occupation: Manager of a community centre

If you had to be a Disney character at Disneyworld for a day, who would you choose to be?

Syndrome from The Incredibles.

How much money do you think you've spent over the course of your life so far?

£100,000 at least!

Would you rather give to your neighbour or to someone living in a developing nation?

To my neighbour.

Why?

Because it can be a lifelong commitment and not just a one-off gift.

What did Jesus teach us about giving?

That everything we have is God's and that our life is a continual offering to him. So we should be using everything we have and everything we do for his glory.

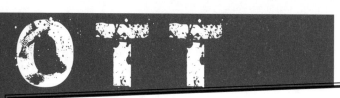

One of the Pharisees asked Jesus to eat with him. Jesus went into the Pharisee's house and took a place at the table.

There was a sinful woman in that town. She knew that Jesus was eating at the Pharisee's house. So the woman brought some expensive perfume in an alabaster jar. She stood at Jesus' feet, crying. Then she began to wash his feet with her tears. She dried his feet with her hair. She kissed his feet many times and rubbed them with the perfume.

When the Pharisee who asked Jesus to come to his house saw this, he said to himself, 'If this man were a prophet, he would know that the woman who is touching him is a sinner!'

In reply to what the Pharisee was thinking, Jesus said, 'Simon, I have something to say to you.'

Simon said, 'Let me hear it, Teacher.'

Jesus said, 'There were two men. Both men owed money to the same banker. One man owed him 500 silver coins. The other man owed him 50 silver coins. The men had no money, so they could not pay their debt. But the banker told the men that they did not have to pay him. Which one of those two men will love him more?'

Simon answered, 'I think it would be the one who owed him the most money.'

Jesus said to him, 'You are right.' Then he turned to the woman and said to Simon, 'Do you see this woman? When I came into your house, you gave me no water for my feet. But she washed my feet with her tears and dried my feet with her hair. You did not greet me with a kiss, but she has been kissing my feet since I came in. You did not honour me with oil for my head, but she rubbed my feet with her sweet-smelling oil. I tell you that her many sins are forgiven. This is clear, because she showed great love. People who are forgiven only a little will love only a little.'

Then Jesus said to her, 'Your sins are forgiven.'

The people sitting at the table began to think to themselves, 'Who does this man think he is? How can he forgive sins?'

Jesus said to the woman, 'Because you believed, you are saved from your sins. Go in peace.'

(Luke 7:36–50)

For me, this story is a beautiful picture of unbridled worship. This woman does not care who else is in the room. She simply desires to pour all her love in the direction of this one man. The word used here for 'kiss' means 'to kiss fondly, to caress' or to 'kiss again and again'. The image of her washing his feet with her tears is so beautiful that we forget that this means she must also have been crying in Jesus' presence. This is surely an appropriate response to the love that is forgiving her.

Where did we learn that we should suppress our emotions in worship? Certainly not in the Bible. How I long for this kind of freedom in worship. What a contrast to the Pharisees, who are doing everything by the book, but failing to show any real hospitality.

ARE WE MORE CONCERNED WITH WHAT PEOPLE AROUND US WILL THINK AND WHAT IS 'PROPER' THAN GIVING OUR ALL TO JESUS?

The extravagance of his love to us demands an extravagant response. When

was the last time you were extravagant in your love of God? When was the last time you really went over-the-top? Or are you inhibited by some Pharisees, or the 'Pharisee' in yourself?

You have been forgiven much. None of us in this world have been forgiven 'little', so we don't have that as an opt-out clause.

FIND A WAY TO EXPRESS YOUR LOVE TO GOD EXTRAVAGANTLY. This may be with a massive painting or sculpture, a really loud song, a long night on the dance floor with hands in the air, or a big donation to your church.

Now make plans to bless a brother or sister with an extravagant gift. Something that doesn't necessarily make any sense, either to your bank balance or to your schedule, but something that will bless them beyond belief. This may be replacing a broken appliance, or buying them tickets to a concert, or flights to Paris. When did Jesus ever say 'Blessed are the measured'?

Andy Flannagan, *God 360°*, **Spring Harvest and Authentic Media, 2006**

Reaction Reaction Reaction Reaction

CIRCLE:

😊 🙁 😐 😯 😕 😮

TICK:

Total rubbish ☐   Not sure ☐   Worth thinking about ☐   Genius ☐

FILL:

....

....

....

....

Take It All

Ever been in a worship service singing one of those 'I give it all to you/You're all I need, Jesus' kind of worship songs and felt a bit uncomfortable because you weren't quite sure you really meant it? I was at an amazing worship and prayer event recently singing my heart out and it came to one of those lines: 'Take it all – just give me Jesus'!

To start with, I just tried to avoid singing that line, but then it kept being repeated, so in a moment of being really honest with God I sang it and then in my head I added, ' . . . except for the new house that we're buying, and my kids'. I felt bad for saying it, for not really being able to say I would give it all away, but then I just felt God smile and I laughed. I realized that God would far rather I were honest with him in my worship than to say the 'right things'. Let's be frank, getting to a place where we could lose everything and just have Christ and be OK is not that easy. I felt that God was saying, 'Thanks for being honest for once! And by the way, I know you need those things – they're great and I don't want you to give them up.'

I'm not saying there won't come a time where you'll have to sacrificially give, and where you will have to walk away from things or people that you value and just cling to God. I've had those moments too. But sometimes we can forget that God actually wants good things for us and wants to bless us.

The song I was singing went on to say that all my devotion belongs to Jesus. As I sang that, the penny dropped. That's how we get to a point of being able to say, 'Take it all – just give me Jesus'. As a consequence of devoting ourselves to him our values change. The stuff we can't live without changes. We get to a place where all we truly want is Jesus, and where we value time with him and relationship with him over everything else. **THE 'STUFF' THE WORLD OFFERS US BECOMES LESS VALUABLE THAN PLEASING HIM.** I'm definitely not there yet, but I'm excited to understand the way to get there, and it's simple, like so many things in our Christian life. We just devote ourselves to Jesus, and then he changes us and gets us there. But in the meantime, I reckon being honest with him is a good place to start!

Are there things (or people) that if you are really honest you would struggle to give up?

....
....
....
....

What are some ways you could devote yourself to Jesus?

....
....
....
....

ReactionReactionReactionReaction

CIRCLE:

TICK:

Total rubbish ☐   Not sure ☐   Worth thinking about ☐   Genius ☐

FILL:

....
....
....
....

Who Owns Who?

Chip talks

When the big boss at MTV was asked the question, 'What is it like to know that your company has so much influence on this generation?' his reply was simple: 'MTV doesn't influence this generation. MTV *owns* this generation.'

There is a subtle yet profound difference between something (or someone) merely influencing us and that same thing 'owning' us. When it comes to our money, we need to make sure we've got it the right way around – we own the money, the money doesn't own us. The proof is in the decisions we make and the considerations we factor in to those decisions. Here are a few examples:

You're just about to finish work, when your boss offers to pay you £20 to stay and do an extra hour of overtime. It sounds like a great idea, until your closest friend in the world sends you a text asking you to meet them. It's urgent and you know that they need you as a shoulder to cry on. What are you going to do? Who demands the most loyalty from you? How important is that £20 anyway?

Or . . .

You've saved up £3,000 to go on a gap year 'mission trip' to a developing country. After working hard at a part-time job and saving every penny for more than five months, the time has come to write a cheque for the full amount. This is the moment you've been looking forward to for a very long time, and yet you can't shake the thought that there are so many other things you could spend this money on – after all, you've earned it yourself. Do you go ahead and write the cheque? What are your real priorities? What are the eternal consequences of going to that developing country versus not going?

In either of these scenarios, **IF THE MONEY COMES FIRST THEN, UNFORTUNATELY, YOUR MONEY OWNS YOU**. If, however, you're able to put your friends and/or missions work first, then you are exhibiting a more mature approach to the situation, and you're proving that you are not owned by money.

In Luke 16:1–15, we find a very interesting story told by Jesus himself, which clearly outlines the same principle. Why not take a few minutes to read it for yourself? Then answer these questions:

- How was the shrewd manager proving that money wasn't his chief incentive?

- Who are the two masters Jesus is referring to?

- What was the Pharisees' response? Which 'master' were they choosing to follow?

Reaction Reaction Reaction Reaction

CIRCLE:

😊   🙁   😐   😮   😕   😲

TICK:

Total rubbish ☐   Not sure ☐   Worth thinking about ☐   Genius ☐

FILL:

....

....

....

....

Pin the Cheque on the Donkey

In recent years, charities have faced some difficult times. There's talk of recession and wars, worry and house prices, job security and pensions – and all of that makes people less likely to give to charity. They want to hang onto their hard-earned cash for themselves. But there's one charity that doesn't seem to have to worry about money – the Donkey Sanctuary in Devon. Last year they were given more than Age UK and the Samaritans combined.

The Donkey Sanctuary was set up by a woman called Elisabeth Svendsen in 1969 after she got her first donkey called Naughty Face. Now the Sanctuary looks after thousands of donkeys on its farm and has many more in its donkey-fostering scheme. These are looked after by families around the UK who are able to meet the high standards of accommodation required. The Donkey Sanctuary look after nearly three-quarters of the UK donkey population and it means we have probably the best looked-after donkeys in the world!

People in Britain are well known for giving more to animal charities than to charities for the disabled or the elderly. 'When people make disparaging comments about animal charities, what they are making disparaging comments about really is the British public,' says Tom Monk who works for a charity marketing group. 'What's quite hard to swallow is the fact that **LOTS OF PEOPLE OUT THERE WOULD RATHER GIVE MONEY AND SYMPATHY TO DONKEYS** than to, for example, the children of refugees or other hard to support causes.'

- Why do you think so many people give money to The Donkey Sanctuary and to other animal charities? Why are they less likely to give money to charities working with refugees and asylum seekers?

- What charities have you given money to, or raised money for? Why did you decide to support that charity?

- What reasons or excuses do people have for not giving to charity? How would you answer those excuses?

- Why do Christians think giving is an important thing to do?

Jenny Baker, *Vibrant Spirituality*, Spring Harvest and Authentic Media, 2004

Reaction Reaction Reaction Reaction

CIRCLE:

TICK:

Total rubbish ☐   Not sure ☐   Worth thinking about ☐   Genius ☐

FILL:

....
....
....
....

Reality Check

PUT YOUR MONEY WHERE YOUR MOUTH IS!

Alright, so in the last reality check we worked out how much money you were spending on essentials and non-essentials (i.e. things you can live without, although it might not always feel like it!).

So, just to recap:

Write down how much money you get every week (pocket money, earnings, benefits):

£.................... (e.g. £5.00)

Just to remind yourself, write down how much you spend on non-essentials:

£.................... (e.g. £3.00)

Now work out what 10% of the first number is (multiply it by 0.1):

£.................... (e.g. £0.50)

Lots of Christians believe that we should give a tithe (10%) of our income back to God as you've read about in this Life Lesson. The number you've just come up with is how much you could give if you gave 10%. So now take your tithe away from the money you spend on non-essentials (the second number):

£....................

This is what you are left with to spend as you like. Of course you can give more than 10%. Some people even give away 90% of their income! But you can see that you still end up with a lot more than you've given away.

If you don't already tithe, write down what you will have to give up in order to give God 10% of your income:

....
....
....
....

Check out the scriptures below and write down in your own words how God responds when we give generously with a cheerful heart:

Luke 6:38

2 Corinthians 9:6–8

....
....
....
....

Is it All About Money?

Tell those who are rich to do good – to be rich in good works. And tell them they should be happy to give and ready to share. By doing this, they will be saving up a treasure for themselves. And that treasure will be a strong foundation on which their future life will be built. They will be able to have the life that is true life.

(1 Timothy 6:18–19)

3

First up

Ever feel a bit like a 12-slice pizza when there are 13 people in the room? Everyone wants a piece of you but there just isn't enough to go around! Your maths teacher wants you to do loads of homework for her, but you know you've also got geography coursework and rehearsals for the performing arts production. On top of all that your church youth group wants you involved in an outreach every other Saturday and at church on Sunday. Your parents want you to visit your nana every week. Your mates want to get together. You feel like there aren't enough hours in the day – and now here we are talking about giving! For some people, giving money isn't the hardest thing – giving up time and energy is a bigger sacrifice. For others, giving away things can be the hardest part of really letting God take control of your life.

What we've found is that a lot comes down to hearing from God and being obedient. We know God has told us to give. This could be money, stuff, time, thoughts, prayers or anything else that costs you something. How much and what, should really come down to you following God's direction. If you try to do it all, you really will end up feeling completely stretched and worn out.

So here's the thing. Take some time to seek God about what else you should be giving – apart from the obvious money stuff. Tithes and offerings are standard, but in what other ways does God want to use you to bless others?

As with giving money, you really need to look at it through God's back-to-front 'kingdom glasses'. Don't think, 'How much will I have to sacrifice?' Think, 'How many opportunities can I have to go on amazing adventures with God and be totally and utterly blessed?' This Life Lesson will hopefully start you thinking about lots of different ways to give that don't necessarily involve your money.

Practise Generosity

Have you ever given a gift – I mean something you REALLY loved, an item you would want yourself – to someone else? It feels so good when you get to see the excitement and happiness on the other person's face.

I absolutely love giving gifts. I always feel so good when I do and definitely receive much more out of giving than I ever do from receiving. Giving is also a very quick 'pick-me-up'. Next time you are feeling a bit low or lost, give a gift to someone who looks like they need one.

Please note that a 'gift' does not have to cost money or even be a physical item that you could put on a shelf. You could write someone an encouraging letter or note. You could offer to baby-sit for a tired mum or dad. You could offer to help someone else study for a test or you could pick your mum some flowers from the garden. **YOU WILL INSTANTLY FEEL GREAT WHEN YOU ARE GENEROUS WITH YOUR THOUGHTS AND TIME**. It also adds deposits into your own self-esteem account because you are giving of yourself.

The law of giving means that you will always receive a return 10 times more than you will ever give. But what you get back will not usually come from the people or places that you expected.

Food for thought . . .

Don't ever keep track of your generosity. The people who constantly keep track of people to whom they have served or blessed are painful. If you are going to expect people to do things for you in return, don't bother! Give without ever expecting.

'Be careful! When you do something good, don't do it in front of others so that they will see you. If you do that, you will have no reward from your Father in heaven.'
(Matthew 6:1)

Sharon Witt, *Teen Talk*, Authentic Media, 2011

ReactionReactionReactionReaction

CIRCLE:

😊 🙁 😐 😮 😕 😲

TICK:

Total rubbish ☐　Not sure ☐　Worth thinking about ☐　Genius ☐

FILL:

....

....

....

....

Top Table

Read Luke 14:7–14

Isn't it funny how some people like to be noticed? How they always want to hog the limelight? This might be you, and on occasions I fear it is me. We need to pay close attention to this story.

When someone invites you to a party, don't take a seat at the top table, for people who are closer to the person throwing the party may well have been invited. If so, the host who invited both of you will come and say to you, 'This place is reserved. Give this person your seat.' By then, not only will you feel humiliated but also the only places left will be right at the back. It is much better when you arrive to take a place at the back. Then when the host sees you he may well say, 'My friend, what are you doing here? Come with me to a better place.' Then he will be honouring you in front of the other guests. For all those who think highly of themselves will be humiliated, but those who humble themselves will be lifted up.

Next time you are having a party do not invite your relatives and friends, because if you do they are bound to ask you back and so you will be repaid. But when you plan your meal invite the unemployed, the elderly and the single parents – then you really will be blessed. Although they will not be able to repay you in kind, you will be blessed in many ways and some of these rewards will last forever.

Be humble

Jesus always encourages us to be humble. Yet it is very easy and quite natural that you want the best things for yourself. That is why there is always a charge for the best seats on the plane or at the theatre. But if we somehow feel that we deserve the best and that we have merited it in some way because of our goodness, we may well be in for a shock. Puffing ourselves up and making ourselves look important can easily rebound on us. If this happens in public we will be humiliated – and everyone likes to see self-important people brought down a peg or two.

Jesus warns us that even if we get away with this on earth, we won't when we stand before him. **WE NEED TO REMEMBER THAT WHATEVER WE HAVE ACHIEVED ON EARTH IS NOT TO DO WITH OUR OWN MERIT**. It is purely a matter of the gifts God has bestowed upon us and the opportunities he has given us. Yet we continue to try to 'move up in the world' and we desperately send out signals to others which seem to say, 'Look at me: I am very important!' We attempt to do this by mixing with the 'right' people, going to the 'right' places and wearing the 'right' clothes. The question we have to ask ourselves is: who are we trying to impress?

Share with others who have less

The second part of the story also hits home. Who do we mix with, and why? Of course we all have friends that we like to be with and whose company we enjoy, but Jesus wants us to go further. It is only natural to ask friends round and go to their homes on occasions, but that is not practising hospitality – it's just us having a good time! **WHAT WE ARE BEING ASKED TO DO IS EXTEND OUR GENEROSITY AND GIVING FURTHER**. We need to try to baby-sit for the single parent who otherwise would never get out of the house, spend time with the widower and smile at the stranger. Offer to buy a sandwich for those we see begging for food on our streets. These things, which may seem minor to us, can actually be an enormous blessing to others in so many ways. The little unexpected kindnesses will be felt by others and will be seen by God.

Keith Tondeur, *Street Parables*, Authentic Media, 2004

ReactionReactionReactionReaction

CIRCLE:

☺ ☹ 😐 ‼ 😕 😮

TICK:

Total rubbish ☐ Not sure ☐ Worth thinking about ☐ Genius ☐

FILL:

....

....

....

....

Hidden pearls

I taught a singing group on a voluntary basis for 20 years. The sopranos were quite weak, so I had to sing very loudly. The Lord gave me my voice, and I was glad to be able to use it to help people, but I think I wore it out with too much singing!

Volunteer Your Time

When I started teaching, there were no paid positions available at the school I had attended as a teenager. It was my favourite school and I really wanted to work there. So I chose to volunteer my time two days every week, just to gain teaching experience. I really enjoyed those times and it reinforced to me that teaching was the profession I wanted to follow. Before long, I was offered casual work within the school. I gained a full-time position the following year because I had experience within the school and they knew me, by then, quite well.

In giving back to others, think about perhaps volunteering your time to help out others. Or consider working for specific organizations. Many places rely on volunteers to keep them operational. Not only does volunteering help out others, but the benefits to you can be immeasurable.

VOLUNTEERING INCREASES OUR SELF-ESTEEM BECAUSE WE BUILD OURSELVES UP WHEN WE HELP OUT OTHERS.

At a youth forum I attended, a teenager aged 18 got up to talk about his experiences in volunteering. He was 12 years old when he first began offering to help in a care home for the elderly. He really enjoyed his time there and made many friends while gaining valuable work experience.

When he decided to apply for a job at a major fast-food outlet, he wasn't alone. More than 700 young people had put their names down for about three positions. He thought he had no hope at all because he had never had a paid part-time job before. 'What chance have I got?' he thought.

The employers picked him. They had seen something he had missed in his moments of doubt – all the experience he had gained while volunteering at the care home. The skills he built up over six years had included working with people, problem solving, commitment to the position and residents, diligence and teamwork.

Think about some of the areas that you are interested in pursuing as a career when you leave school. Consider approaching some businesses in your area that relate to your interests. Many people in positions of importance began by volunteering their time. And don't think any job is beneath you.

Remember, everyone has to start somewhere. If you have to make coffee and clean up after other people just so you can be around when positions become available, then do so! Plenty of people began their careers as coffee servers who did so with a smile on their face and a 'can do' attitude.

Sharon Witt, *Teen Talk*, Authentic Media, 2011

Reaction Reaction Reaction Reaction

CIRCLE:

☺ ☹ 😐 😦 😕 😲

TICK:

Total rubbish ☐   Not sure ☐   Worth thinking about ☐   Genius ☐

FILL:

....
....
....
....

Neighbours

Read Luke 10:25–37

Many religious people are anxious to find the right formula to ensure that their behaviour and good works gain them eternal life. We know that the Bible clearly says we should love God and our neighbour as much as we love ourselves, and Jesus tells us that through doing this we will have eternal life. But are we really doing this? Take a look at the following story. It might just prompt a bit of self-analysis!

A young girl was coming home from a late-night party rather the worse for wear. She was assaulted, beaten, mugged and left in the entrance to an alley.

A liberal churchman was going down the main road on the way to church, and when he saw her he passed by on the other side. He was hurrying to a debate about one-hundred-and-one ways to find God.

An evangelical also passed by on the other side. He could not possibly be late for his church service, as a few new converts from Alpha could be attending.

But a barman from a club saw her and felt pity for her. He stopped his car, went over to her and helped clean up her wounds. He drove her to a nearby hotel he knew of, where he asked the manager to look after her and give her a bed and a good meal. He gave the hotel manager his credit card details and told him to charge all the expenses to it . . .

If we were asked which of the three men was a good neighbour to the young girl, I am sure we would all say that it was the man who was kind to her. In other words, we are talking about the one who actually did something about her plight.

Jesus clearly agrees with this message. This is correct teaching. We need to look behind the label. We need to show our Christian love and compassion to everyone we come across.

Be compassionate

As Christians, we can find that our positions and deeply held beliefs sometimes deflect us from kindnesses. Our determination to keep our passions under control can mean that we also stifle our compassion. It is easy to justify ourselves when situations like this occur, but Jesus is saying to us, 'Hold on a moment. Put yourself in the shoes of the young woman. How grateful you would be to anyone who helped you. **REMEMBER: BUT FOR THE GRACE OF GOD IT COULD BE YOU LYING THERE IN THE GUTTER.'**

Why not do that for a moment? Imagine you are the man beaten up by the robbers in Luke 10, or think about how you would feel if you were that young girl who had just been attacked . . . All the young woman wants is to be helped. She will be very grateful to anyone passing by who stops and comes to her assistance. It is quite likely that as she gets to know more about her rescuer she will start to ask questions: 'Why did you stop?' 'Why have you given up time and money for me?' 'What motivates you to be so kind?'

Keith Tondeur, *Street Parables*, Authentic Media, 2004

Reaction Reaction Reaction Reaction

CIRCLE:

TICK:
Total rubbish ☐   Not sure ☐   Worth thinking about ☐   Genius ☐

FILL:

....

....

....

....

Good Work

(This extract is all about work but you can apply it to school or college too.)

Read this passage in your place of work. Get in early if you have to:

> When all the people were being baptized, Jesus came and was baptized too. And while he was praying, the sky opened, and the Holy Spirit came down on him. The Spirit looked like a real dove. Then a voice came from heaven and said, 'You are my Son, the one I love. I am very pleased with you.'

(Luke 3:21–22)

God spoke these words before Jesus began his ministry. So his expression of pleasure is not based on healings, preaching and teaching, but on Jesus' character of simple service, working with his father Joseph. The Greek word *teknon* that is normally translated 'carpenter' can also be translated as something more akin to an 'odd-job' man. Can you imagine Jesus coming round to fix your light fittings, sort out your boiler, or clean out your shed? Take this on board today as encouragement for the sometimes mundane service of your work. To you it may not feel significant but note Colossians 3:23:

> In all the work you are given, do the best you can. Work as though you are working for the Lord, not any earthly master.

It is all too easy to disconnect our 'spiritual' lives from our work. But **WORK IS NOT JUST WHAT WE HAVE TO DO TO SURVIVE. IT IS A GOD-ORDAINED ACT OF WORSHIP**, a huge percentage of what we are on the earth to do. God was and is the ultimate worker. His work in creation set a pattern for our lives.

See if you can hear his voice over the hum of the photocopier today – 'I am very pleased with you.'

Take time today to encourage one or all of your workmates, and let them know that they are doing a great job. With a little bit of preparation, what about leaving a little postcard (perhaps with a chocolate) on everyone's desk

(or somewhere appropriate) pointing out something that you appreciate about them. You will change their day. You will struggle to find something positive to say about some people. Fighting hard to find these things is an important discipline. There is always something you can find. We just need to make the effort to find it. Writing people off is the world's way, not ours.

Andy Flannagan, *God 360°*, Spring Harvest and Authentic Media, 2006

ReactionReactionReactionReaction

CIRCLE:

😊 ☹️ 😐 😗 😕 😮

TICK:

Total rubbish ☐   Not sure ☐   Worth thinking about ☐   Genius ☐

FILL:

....

....

....

....

Say Thank You,
Often :)

Question: How much does it cost you to say 'thank you' to someone?

Answer: Absolutely nothing!

One of the simplest principles of being thankful is so very often overlooked or forgotten. Say it!

Something that I really appreciate about my students is that they will often say 'thank you' to me at the end of a drama lesson. Whilst it costs nothing for students to thank me, it means a great deal to me because it shows that the person appreciates the effort I have put in to preparing a lesson.

Next time you step off a bus, thank the bus driver; that driver has reached your destination safely. If a teacher hands you back an exam or assignment that has been marked, say thank you because personal time has gone into marking it for you.

Sharon Witt, *Teen Talk*, Authentic Media, 2011

Reaction ReactionReactionReaction

CIRCLE:

TICK:

Total rubbish ☐   Not sure ☐   Worth thinking about ☐   Genius ☐

FILL:

....

....

....

....

Supermarket
SWEEP

I'm always looking out for areas of our lives where we can give God more access, especially if they are areas where we don't normally think about him. This is an example.

> Truth, wisdom, learning and understanding are worth paying money for. They are worth far too much to ever sell.
>
> *(Proverbs 23:23)*

How much praying or God awareness is going on when you're in the supermarket? When those automatic doors slide open, are you purely and simply in 'task mode'? If he prompted you to speak to someone, or help someone, would you be in a place to hear? Or are you tunnel-visioned like I often am? Do you become a bargain hunter with little thought for your health or the health of food producers around the world? Is God there in your trolley or whimpering in the car like a forgotten puppy?

GOD WANTS US TO SHARE EVERY PART OF OUR LIVES WITH HIM, so I know God wants us to enjoy shopping with him. There is real freedom in talking to God (privately) in a public place, and much thankfulness can be conveyed for what greets our eyes. Can you believe the diversity of foodstuffs that are presented to us these days? Sometimes I simply love looking at them all, without the slightest intention of purchasing. I'm thinking, 'God, thank you so much for all this provision. We are so blessed.'

So, pray your way around the aisles . . . giving thanks for the products and praying for the parts of the world represented by them. Pray for those folks who suffer greatly in developing countries to give us the luxury of cheap food. Give thanks that you have money to spend. Speak to the store management, asking that they stock products with the 'Fairtrade' mark. These days it goes far beyond bananas and chocolate. You can keep up to date with what produce is available via www.fairtrade.org.uk.

If you feel you need to push an empty trolley around with you to get into the vibe, then go for it. If you actually need stuff, then feel free to grab. Hopefully, the next time you're back your praying self will have more of a chance of kicking in.

You could apply this thought to all types of shopping. Or would God ask us too many awkward questions like, 'Do you really need this or do you simply want it?' **WHEN DID WE START BELIEVING THAT 'RETAIL THERAPY' WAS DETACHABLE FROM OUR SPIRITUAL LIVES?** Once you get home, show Jesus around your house as a kind of 'virtual estate agent'. Do every room. How would you explain the need for everything that he finds? Are we countercultural or merely clinging to the culture of the counter?

Andy Flannagan, *God 360°*, Spring Harvest and Authentic Media, 2006

Reaction ReactionReactionReaction

CIRCLE:

😊 😞 😐 😮 😕 😲

TICK:

Total rubbish ☐ Not sure ☐ Worth thinking about ☐ Genius ☐

FILL:

....

....

....

....

Give a precious item that you own to a local charity shop or 'cash converters' store. It doesn't need to be something expensive – just something that has sentimental value to you or will be hard to replace. If you're struggling to think of anything, just have a quick look around your bedroom, living room or, for the most effective method, ask a friend to choose. They'll know what will really mean something to you. If you're still really struggling, as a soft option, you could just choose your favourite CD or DVD.

In the next one to two days, experience what it felt like for God to 'let go' of us, running the risk that we may never return. We enjoy having free will, but anyone who is a parent will tell you that, at times, you would rather cancel your offspring's free will for a day or two, to save them from themselves. However, the remarkable truth is that the story doesn't end there. God buys us back.

Walk to the shop for the second time, mirroring God's 'rescue mission', and as you do, ask God to reveal to you the scale of his love for his children who have not yet returned.

You won't know whether your item will still be there, or whether it will have been snaffled up by a bargain hunter. Experience the tension. **THIS IS THE TENSION THAT GOD MUST EXPERIENCE IN GIVING US FREE WILL.** As you buy the item back you might experience a sense of injustice in having to pay for something that is actually yours, but that is what God did for us.

> Christ entered the Most Holy Place only once – enough for all time. He entered the Most Holy Place by using his own blood, not the blood of goats or young bulls. He entered there and made us free from sin forever.

(Hebrews 9:12)

It is this 'redemption' that we have been fleshing out here. In these days of multiple kidnappings, we are sadly all too aware of what a ransom is. It is quite literally given in exchange for someone's life. The money you paid in the exercise above was a ransom for your precious item. With the item safe in your possession, reflect on the fact that God's economy doesn't allow for simple cash conversion. **THE CURRENCY OF THIS TRANSACTION IS BLOOD.**

If the item has been snapped up by an avid One Direction fan, then you are going to experience something of the pain of the father of the prodigal son who let his son depart with half the inheritance. Let this longing to have what was once yours safely restored change your heart and prayers for those who you know are still 'in a faraway land'. If we even knew a fraction of his pain, I think it would change our praying lives forever.

Andy Flannagan, *God 360°*, Spring Harvest and Authentic Media, 2006

Reaction ReactionReactionReaction

CIRCLE:

☺ ☹ 😐 😮 🙂 😲

TICK:

Total rubbish ☐   Not sure ☐   Worth thinking about ☐   Genius ☐

FILL:

....

....

....

....

Earthly Treasure

They sold their land and the things they owned. Then they divided the money and gave it to those who needed it.

(Acts 2:45)

Why do we attach so much importance to accumulating stuff? We'd like to think we don't, but most of our houses tell a more honest story, with a kitchen appliance or receptacle for every conceivable emergency culinary situation; enough garments to clothe a small town in Finland; enough technology to entertain, inform and distract us from the real world until the year 2035. Jesus is very clear about where our investment should be and has the audacity to link our ability to invest in the Kingdom with our over-the-top desire to invest in our comfort or perceived security here on earth.

So [with the permission or your parents] have a 'life laundry'. Sell off (perhaps via eBay) all the things that, with honest reflection, are simply 'treasures on earth', then invest that cash in some heavenly treasure, be that paying for a friend to have a holiday, sponsoring a child, supporting an aid agency, or enabling your church to make more of an impact in your community.

Doing this is important, but it's also deeper than that. It's not merely about the money. Matthew 6:19–21 says:

'Don't save treasures for yourselves here on earth. Moths and rust will destroy them. And thieves can break into your house and steal them. Instead, save your treasures in heaven, where they cannot be destroyed by moths or rust and where thieves cannot break in and steal them. Your heart will be where your treasure is.'

Our accumulation of stuff or selfish experiences reveals a heart position that is earth-centred. A major reason for this is the way that society has evolved. The sort of heart change and life change that God desires for us is not meant to be possible in the context of individualized lives. Acts 2:42–45 tells us:

The believers spent their time listening to the teaching of the apostles. They shared everything with each other. They ate together and prayed together. Many wonders and miraculous signs were happening through the apostles, and everyone felt great respect for God. All the believers stayed together and shared everything. They sold their land and the things they owned. Then they divided the money and gave it to those who needed it.

HEAVEN-ORIENTED LIVING REQUIRES COMMUNITY AND SHARING.

Could you resolve with another family to share some household appliances or even DVDs/CDs?

Shock – no! We want to be able to use that or watch that whenever we decide to. To paraphrase something that was never true anyway, it would seem that 'handiness is next to godliness'. We want to be in control.

God calls us to another way: the way that doesn't have a TV in every bedroom; the way that shares a lawnmower; the way that pays for someone else's MOT when they can't afford it.

After your decisions, read Luke 12:27–30.

Andy Flannagan, *God 360°*, Spring Harvest and Authentic Media, 2006

Reaction Reaction Reaction Reaction

CIRCLE:

TICK:

Total rubbish ☐ Not sure ☐ Worth thinking about ☐ Genius ☐

FILL:

....
....
....
....

Name: **Mwila Mulenshi**

Age: **24**

Town: **London**

Occupation: **Programme co-ordinator**

P E O P L E   C L I P

If you could close your eyes and be anywhere in the world right now, where would you be?

Not in a geographical location but in the centre of the will of God, with my husband.

If you could break a world record, which would you break?

First black woman to be policy advisor for education.

Who is the most generous person you know?

Ebru Gursoy, my best friend.

What's the best thing you can give away?

My time, because it's so precious to me and I love 'me' time.

Most Valuable

Chip talks

Theophrastus, a Greek philosopher who lived 300 years before Jesus, said this: 'Time is the most valuable thing a man can spend.' But I have to say, although I can see where he's coming from with that statement, I'm not entirely sure I agree with him.

In my opinion, the most valuable thing I can ever spend (or give) is my heart. Check out what these few verses say about how much emphasis God puts on the importance of giving your heart:

'You must love the LORD your God with all your heart, with all your soul and with all your strength.'
(Deuteronomy 6:5)

'You will search for me, and when you search for me with all your heart, you will find me.'
(Jeremiah 29:13)

'God doesn't look at what people see. People judge by what is on the outside, but the LORD looks at the heart.'
(1 Samuel 16:7)

When I give my heart to someone or something, I'm giving the best I have to offer. I'm putting my blood, sweat and tears into it. I'm not just spending my time, but also my thoughts, energy and every resource at my disposal on that person or thing I'm giving my heart to. My heart is precious to me, so I'm not going to waste it in superficial frivolity.

Take a moment to stop and think about who or what you're giving your heart to right now. **IF WHAT THE BIBLE SAYS IS TRUE, THEN THAT IS THE MOST VALUABLE ASSET YOU POSSESS.** Choosing what you invest your heart and soul in is certainly not a decision to be taken lightly. If you're serious about this, find a quiet place, close your eyes, and ask God to search your heart. Ask him to reveal to you where your true allegiance lies. You may want to write some things down on paper or type them into your phone. Then, as and when you are ready to submit those things to him, give Jesus your heart – every last part of it. After all, that is the safest, most secure place it could ever be.

Reaction Reaction Reaction Reaction

CIRCLE:

😊 ☹️ 😐 😮 😟 😲

TICK:

Total rubbish ☐   Not sure ☐   Worth thinking about ☐   Genius ☐

FILL:

....
....
....
....

Give Away

A few years back Chip and I were at a big summer Bible conference. Meetings in cowsheds, camping in the rain, dodgy toilets – you know the drill! Anyway, one night we went to the usual evening meeting and sat down to listen to the preacher. The guy started speaking and then, about halfway through his talk, asked everyone to look under their chairs for an envelope. We all bent down, picked up a little white envelope and opened it as instructed. Inside each envelope was a crisp, shiny, £10 note. Wow, that was a surprise! Now this wasn't just a small gathering of people, there were thousands and thousands of people in the room.

The speaker went on to explain that he had re-mortgaged his house in order to fund this little experiment! He was raising money for a charity and instead of just asking everyone to give their money he had decided to switch things around and give everyone a tenner. He then explained that he wanted every person in the room to take that ten-pound note and try and make it grow and then send in any money they made in the next few months, or return the tenner! He suggested loads of ideas, getting together with a group of others and then putting £100 into buying equipment to provide a service like cleaning services or car washing, buying cake ingredients and selling cakes. Obviously there are endless possibilities. What an amazing idea!

Firstly it was amazing that the preacher was so passionate about his cause that he was prepared to risk losing a lot of his own personal money in order to raise money for charity. I didn't really think many people would just pocket it and not give it back on purpose, but you know how things go. You put it in your wallet with good intentions and then need some cash for something, forget to put it back, or forget to send it in. That's fine for one person – but imagine if a thousand people did that with your money!

I realized that **WE DON'T NEED A LOT OF MONEY TO START OFF WITH IN ORDER TO MAKE A DIFFERENCE.** Over the next few months there were loads of stories of how people turned their £10 notes into more money and the man's charity eventually ended up with hundreds of thousands of pounds. You or I could do the same thing at any point. Next time you are asked for money, how about instead of just giving £10, you commit to take a month and try and turn £10 into £100! As well as creating more wealth to give, you will be learning useful skills and potentially building friendships and awareness of the charity you are creating money for.

ReactionReactionReactionReaction

CIRCLE:

☺ ☹ 😐 😮 😌 😧

TICK:

Total rubbish ☐   Not sure ☐   Worth thinking about ☐   Genius ☐

FILL:

....
....
....
....

Reality Check

WHO TO GIVE TO?

Maybe you are thinking that you want to give more than you used to. You might want to start a regular tithe to your church, or you might want to start giving a bit more than you already do regularly, or maybe you want to make a one-off gift to a person or organization.

Spend some time praying and asking God who you should give to.

Write down what you come up with:

....

....

....

....

If you need any ideas, then how about:

- Getting together with others and sponsoring a child?

- Giving to your local church?

- Giving to a ministry working in your city or elsewhere?

- Sponsoring a Christian worker regularly to help them continue in their ministry?

Maybe you would love to give but you feel that you just don't have the resources. Spend some time praying about how you could creatively raise money to give. Write down any ideas that pop in to your head:

....

....

....

....

Here are some suggestions:

See if you can get someone to give you a small amount (£10 or £20) and then set up a micro-business to make the money grow (e.g. making and selling cakes or cards).

Hire yourself out as a slave for an hourly rate and give the money away – you could babysit, clean, garden, decorate or whatever else is asked of you.

What do you love to do? Could you do it for sponsorship, e.g. a sponsored 10-hour danceathon or sponsored run or swim?

Run some kind of tournament and charge a fee to enter. This could be a sports activity, or even a computer game tournament or game played on your phone.

It's Not Just What You Give, It's the Way You Live!

Good, honest people who refuse to hurt others for money will live through that fire. They refuse to take bribes or listen to plans to murder other people. They refuse to look at plans for doing bad things. They will live safely in high places. They will be protected in high rock fortresses. They will always have food and water.

(Isaiah 33:15–16)

4

First up

So, hopefully by now you've thought a lot about giving and what you should give in terms of your money, time, gifting and possessions, as well as other things. Now we want to take a step back and look at the even bigger picture.

As you read the Bible, there are some things that just keep coming up – things like justice, God's passion for the poor and his hatred of injustice and oppression. The fact is, you can be the most generous person in the world but if your lifestyle is not righteous and full of justice you are kind of missing the point. Here's what Jesus says to the Pharisees in Matthew 23:23: 'It will be bad for you teachers of the law and you Pharisees! You are hypocrites! You give God a tenth of the food you get, even your mint, dill and cumin. But you don't obey the really important teachings of the law – being fair, showing mercy and being faithful. These are the things you should do. And you should also continue to do those other things.'

So, if you are a perfect giver on a Sunday morning and diligently pay your tithe, but you lie about how many hours you worked on your Saturday job, or you ignore the poor, Jesus is saying you've missed it. We often think of the poor as being those people we see around us – homeless people and beggars – but think about how your life impacts the poor around the world. Do the way you shop and the products you buy create poverty for someone else? We are among the most materially blessed people in the world; we have great wealth compared with most of the other inhabitants of earth. But, 'With great power comes great responsibility', as Spider-Man's uncle and aunt are always reminding him. The way we live does impact others – especially those in developing nations.

Read the verse at the start of this Life Lesson again, it's a good one! It is talking about a righteous person and by the sound of it they're the kind of person who runs in the opposite direction to unrighteousness. If you met the person described here, how do you think you would feel?

Contagious Generosity

Chip talks

Chloe was uncomfortable to say the least. It was lunchtime, the clouds had rolled in, and it was clearly about to start chucking down with rain. She rolled her eyes and gave a little shiver. 'I miss my umbrella,' she thought.

F or the past three weeks Chloe had offered to help out with an outdoor soup kitchen, serving the homeless in her community. It was rewarding for her to experience the kindness and gratitude of people she'd normally just walk past on the street. Sometimes she felt as though she came away from these sessions with more than she'd given. Today was different, though. The bad weather had a way of bringing out the worst in people, even the ones who were getting a free hot meal. **NOT A SINGLE SOUL HAD STOPPED AND TAKEN THE TIME TO LOOK HER IN THE EYE AND SAY, 'THANK YOU'.**

Earlier that day, when Chloe was dropping her little brother off at school, she'd noticed that he had forgotten to bring an umbrella. 'Here you go,' she said. 'You can borrow mine.' Now, as the heavens opened and the rain began to pour down, she was beginning to regret that decision.

Finally, Chloe felt she'd had enough. She closed her eyes tight and prayed, 'Dear God, please make the rain stop.' And almost immediately, it did! Or so it seemed. In reality, a homeless man wearing a plastic poncho had walked up behind her with an umbrella and was now holding it above her head. Chloe was so thankful she nearly kissed him. But the man just passed her the umbrella, smiled and walked away.

GENUINE HEARTFELT GENEROSITY IS CONTAGIOUS. When someone blesses us, our natural instinct is to pass on that kindness to others as well. It has a sort of knock-on effect that in the end creates a win–win situation all round.

Check out these amazing words that God gave the prophet Isaiah thousands of years ago. They're just as relevant for us today as they were for the children of Israel back then:

'I want you to share your food with the hungry. I want you to find the poor who don't have homes and bring them into your own homes. When you see people who have no clothes, give them your clothes! Don't hide from your relatives when they need help.' If you do these things, your light will begin to shine like the light of dawn. Then your wounds will heal. Your 'Goodness' will walk in front of you, and the Glory of the LORD will come following behind you.

(Isaiah 58:7–8)

Reaction ReactionReactionReaction

CIRCLE:

TICK:

Total rubbish ☐   Not sure ☐   Worth thinking about ☐   Genius ☐

FILL:

....

....

....

....

Are You a Shopaholic?

Helen talks

We are all pretty much surrounded by opportunities to spend money on ourselves all the time. Corner shops, fast food outlets, coffee shops, adverts on your mobile phone, email deals sent to your computer, adverts on social media, the list is endless. Long gone are the days when you could only spend money between 9 a.m. and 5 p.m. Monday to Saturday in a shop. Now you can rack up bills buying stuff and games on your mobile phone, downloading music and movies, or just shopping online any time of the day or night. The temptation to make impulse buys or to be swayed by what retailers want you to do or buy is everywhere, all the time.

Do you know how much you spend every week? Do you know how much you waste each week on disposable stuff like apps, music and games or food, drinks and snacks that you don't really need? How often you buy something just because an advertiser pushed it in your face?

A few years ago a guy in China called Wang Hao challenged people to live on £10 a week in order to get a grip on their spending on frivolous things and embrace a simpler lifestyle. The challenge didn't take into account any accommodation or regular bills, so most people ended up spending a lot more than £10 a week, but it did help them realize how much they usually spent on food, drinks, entertainment and unnecessary bits and bobs in a week. Over 100,000 people in China took the challenge and many of them couldn't manage it.

How about trying it yourself? Or maybe try £5 if you think £10 would be too easy. **THERE ARE MILLIONS OF PEOPLE IN THE WORLD WHO LIVE ON LESS THAN £10 PER WEEK** including everything: food, clothing, accommodation, even transport. Maybe taking the challenge will help you think about and pray for those people whilst making you aware of how much you consume.

Another initiative is 'Buy Nothing Day'. This is a day, usually the last Saturday in November, where people all over the developed world commit to buying nothing. Buy Nothing Day started off in Canada in the late 90s and has spread worldwide. It's a protest against consumerism and the fact that in the developed world we have only 20% of the world's population yet we consume 80% of the world's resources. It's a day to step back from stuff, stuff, stuff and think about how our lifestyle and buying choices affect others across the globe and the environment. Why not try joining in with Buy Nothing Day, or hold your own day (or couple of days) at some other point this year to try it out. Obviously all shopping isn't bad, but it's good to do a quick shopping detox sometimes to reassess our priorities.

MY PROMISE:

I commit to live on £10/£5 a week from . . . . (date) to . . . . (date)

Write some of the things you have learned through the process:

I will have a 'Buy Nothing Day' on . . . . (date)

How was it?

Reaction ReactionReactionReaction

CIRCLE:

TICK:

Total rubbish ☐   Not sure ☐   Worth thinking about ☐   Genius ☐

FILL:

....

....

Name: **Ebru Gursoy**

Age: **23**

Town: **London**

Occupation: **Singer, songwriter and performer**

Do you have any recurring dreams?

Yes. Of suitcases, long roads and swimming in clean water. God often gives me a word through a man of God in my dreams.

If you could have a super power, what would it be? Why?

My super power would be to be able to see the whole future, read minds and become invisible.

What's the worst gift you've ever been given?

A terrible nightgown which looked like a long piece of cloth!

What's the best gift you've ever been given?

Really meaningful birthday cards.

Shop Till You Drop

Jesus is not opposed to personal property. Christians should not be banned from shopping. But in a culture where shopping and possessions have become the gods of many people around us, we need a new approach to shopping. Jesus' teaching on money and possessions is particularly difficult for us to swallow and we need to recognize the battle between commitment and disposability, compassion and desire, contentment and dissatisfaction. Our last purchase will inevitably be our own coffin and our last will and testament will ultimately give all we own away free of charge. Jesus made the point very clear in the story of the man who received a windfall, bought bigger barns and whose life was held accountable before God within twenty-four hours. We need to learn to spend ourselves in worship to God and for the benefit of others in this life.

Look back over last month's bank statements and evaluate your purchases. What did you buy that you needed? What did you buy that you wanted? What did you buy on impulse? What did you buy for somebody else? **WHAT WOULD JESUS SAY ABOUT YOUR BANK STATEMENT?** Would you be embarrassed if your neighbour saw it, or a church pastor from a developing country saw it? How could you have better spent or saved your money?

Check that the advertisers are not influencing your decisions. Avoid designer labels if possible. Thank God for the products you buy. Be generous and buy something for somebody else. Recognize those in need around you – buy the *Big Issue* or put your change in the charity boxes . . . Buy items that are fairly traded. Avoid items with superfluous amounts of packaging. Refuse or recycle plastic carrier bags. Fix things occasionally, or Freecycle them. Fast from shopping – one day a week, one weekend a month or one month of the year.

Think of your most recent purchases. Which of these (if any) did you buy because it helped define the image you wanted to portray to the world?

Christ purchased us at great expense. What can we do to delight more in this than in things we are able to buy for ourselves?

What do you think the secret of contentment really is? How would this translate into your own personal shopping habits?

Krish Kandiah, *Twenty-Four: Integrating Faith and Real Life*, Authentic Media, 2008

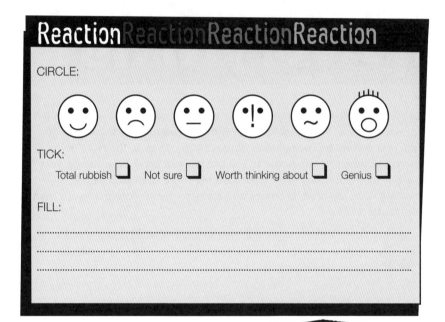

Reaction Reaction Reaction Reaction

CIRCLE:

TICK:

Total rubbish ☐   Not sure ☐   Worth thinking about ☐   Genius ☐

FILL:

....
....
....

A Disciple is Ready to Say Goodbye to Everything

Eyes to the left and the message on a poster hits you: 'It is the same for each of you. You must leave everything you have to follow me. If not, you cannot be my follower' (Luke 14:33). Eyes to the right and there's another: 'If you come to me but will not leave your family, you cannot be my follower. You must love me more than your father, mother, wife, children, brothers and sisters – even more than your own life' (Luke 14:26).

But surely Jesus doesn't want you to sell everything down to your underwear and, for good measure, to launch a hate campaign on those you love the most? You're right, he doesn't. Jesus is using a style of Jewish speech that exaggerates something to the point of unreality to drive home a point. He did much the same with stories about people who had planks in their eyes and camels going through the eyehole of a needle. But the points he makes are still big ones. He wants would-be disciples to understand two more vital things.

He's more important than anything we own

There is nothing worth clinging on to if it keeps us from following him. That's the message. Disciples are asked to have the same attitude to life as their master. Jesus owned heaven and all its splendour. But, for our sake, he chose to die to all it offered. **INSTEAD OF CLINGING ON TO HIS RIGHTS AS GOD, HE WILLINGLY BECAME A MAN, HUMBLING HIMSELF TO DIE ON A CROSS.**

Jesus, who was rich beyond all our understanding, became poor so that we who are bankrupt could have his riches. All he had left in his hands were the nails that provide our forgiveness. When what we own conflicts with following him, there is only one choice on offer.

He is more important than anyone we know

We are to love him so much it would almost seem to others that they were hated. Let me allow Joseph to describe what this meant for him. He puts it this way:

In the Jewish home where I grew up, my family and I were very close. My relationships were so fulfilling – especially with my parents. We loved each other so, so much. Then, at the time when a young man and a father are growing closer, I became a believer in Jesus. I didn't realize just how this would impact the life of our family – especially the relationship with my father. When I finally got the nerve to tell them about my decision it didn't go down too well – it seemed my new-found faith especially hurt him.

Of course, I wasn't trying to cause anyone pain, it's just that I couldn't deny I'd met a real, living person, whom I knew to be the Messiah I'd always longed for. I suppose my love for Jesus could have been mistaken for an act of rebellion towards my parents or a hatred of my Jewish upbringing. But it wasn't. It was just that I now had a very real relationship with the living God – something I could not, with all integrity, deny. I'm sure I could have handled it all more sensitively. But what had once been a close, sharing relationship with my father, became one of a strained silence for a number of years – causing great sadness for both of us.

Joseph had a choice to make. A costly one. And Jesus warns us that following him may demand the same for us. Following Jesus is not about participating in his causes, cleaning up our act somewhat or showing our face more often on a Sunday. It's about putting our whole life under his control and making him the ultimate ruler of all we are, say and do. How this may work out will be very different for each of us. But the principle remains constant. To be a disciple means only the best will do. In God's terms, our very best is ourselves – all we are and all we have – made totally available to him . . .

Behaving like a disciple doesn't get you to heaven

It's important you don't misread me. **YOU GET NO HEAVENLY BROWNIE POINTS BY DOING ALL THE THINGS A DISCIPLE IS SUPPOSED TO DO.** Yes, the world will be a marginally better place if you act like a disciple. But no, it won't make you any more qualified for heaven than you are already. Being a disciple is not part of the journey towards the cross – it's the road that leads on from there. If you try to behave like a disciple of Jesus in order to earn God's forgiveness you are in for a sore disappointment. The only person you're fooling is you – and your ego. And heaven isn't going to be filled with lots of self-righteous people feeling smug about having the right to be there.

You can grit your teeth and obey everything Jesus taught, do everything he tells us to do and abandon everything you possess. But doing all these things will not give you the deep inner joy that comes from being a true follower of Jesus. Sure, being a disciple is something difficult and demanding. But the discipleship-journey is also marked by a wondrous covenant relationship with God – who gives abundantly more than we will ever need to follow him.

Peter Meadows and Joseph Steinberg, *The Book of Y*, Authentic Media, 2007

Reaction Reaction Reaction Reaction

CIRCLE:

TICK:
Total rubbish ☐   Not sure ☐   Worth thinking about ☐   Genius ☐

FILL:

....

....

....

....

Pray

Lord Jesus, thank you for everything you have given me. Thanks for the opportunities that are available for me and the potential I have to bless those around me. I pray that you would help me to hold lightly to my possessions and money, and to remember that everything comes from you. Help me to be generous to others just like you've been generous to me. Please inspire me with creative, crazy and courageous ways that I can give to others.

In Jesus' name,

Amen.

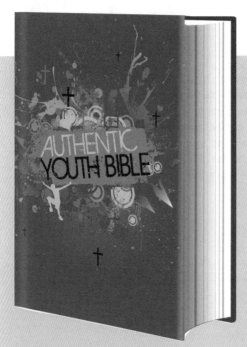

AUTHENTIC YOUTH BIBLE

Red ISBN 978-1-86024-818-4

Teal ISBN 978-1-86024-819-1

YOUTH BIBLE STUDY GUIDES

Sexuality ISBN 978-1-86024-824-5

Following God ISBN 978-1-86024-825-2

Image and Self-Esteem ISBN 978-1-86024-826-9

Peer Pressure ISBN 978-1-86024-827-6

Father God ISBN 978-1-86024-632-6

Jesus Christ and the Holy Spirit ISBN 978-1-86024-633-3

Sin, Forgiveness and Eternal Life ISBN 978-1-86024-634-0

Church, Prayer and Worship ISBN 978-1-86024-635-7

Sharing Your Faith ISBN 978-1-86024-636-4

Tough Times ISBN 978-1-86024-637-1

Money and Giving ISBN 978-1-86024-638-8

Hunger, Poverty and Justice ISBN 978-1-86024-639-5